MW00723474

Scott

Portrait of a Champion

Without Scott Hamilton, figure skating would not be what it is today. In a world where the word "sports" signified groups of men brutally fighting to move a ball, skating was widely regarded as just a novelty event. It was a sport that

produced few heroes and even fewer super-stars. The small handful of skaters who did become famous—such as Peggy Fleming and Dorothy Hamill—were women.

Scott changed that.

When he was a boy, Scott had over-come severe medical problems, exercised hard, and developed himself into an athletic champi-on. Over the years, he continued his diligent practicing, and his dedication paid off when he won the gold medal at the Olympic Games in 1984. Afterward, however, he found it was almost impossible for men to have long careers as a professional skaters. Producers of ice shows were much more interested in hiring pretty women. But Scott would not let this stand in his way. Years before, he had reinvented himself. Now it was time to reinvent his sport.

"My career was at a crossroads and my next move was crucial."

With the help and support of the team at International Management Group (IMG), he created his own professional skating event, a show that became Stars on Ice. Within a few years it became the premiere forum for former Olympic champions. Here they could display their artistry and develop new skills without the restrictions imposed during competition. Here they could turn their sport into a show.

What happened was not only good for Scott but for figure skating itself. The sport

began to draw a whole new audience, and now male skaters could have the same long, fulfilling professional careers and achieve the name recognition that some women skaters had long enjoyed. Skating became a better-known sport, one with its own enduring series of popular heroes and sold-out celebrity tours.

Scott worked tirelessly, skating in the show, serving as a CBS Sports commentator during TV broadcasts, and doing endless charity work for organizations such as the Make-A-Wish Foundation. He became a

hero to many kids who, like Scott when he was younger, suffered from severe medical problems. He made time during  each tour to meet with sick children and, whenever possible, to skate with them.

Then, at the peak of his success, Scott Hamilton unexpectedly faced yet another devastating medical condition—cancer. Once again, he had to fight adversity.

And, once again, he soared.

Scott

His Story

The life of Scott Hamilton begins with an act of warmth and generosity by two very special people, a loving and well-educated Ohio couple who opened the doors of their home—and the doors of their hearts—to a little boy who needed one.

how it all began

Scott Hamilton was born on August 28, 1958, in Bowling Green, Ohio, a mid-sized city just south of the Michigan border. While he was still a baby, Scott was adopted by Ernest and Dorothy Hamilton, who were both teachers at Bowling Green University. The Hamiltons raised Scott as their own, and his childhood was fairly normal until age five, when suddenly his body stopped growing.

This condition baffled his doctors, who at first thought Scott suffered from cystic fibrosis or celiac disease. They also thought he had Schwachman's Syndrome, because he was not correctly digesting food. The  only thing the doctors could tell for certain was that Scott's body did not absorb much nutrition from the meals he ate. Trying to help him, they insisted he try a series of diets, which Scott politely describes

"The more I gave to skating, the more it gave back to me in the form of emotional and physical strength."

as "interesting." Some of the restrictions included forbidding him from having milk or anything made with white flour, including cookies and cake.

These special diets did not work. Scott was no longer growing, and now he was also becoming weaker. He traveled from hospital to hospital,

31

nicknamed it "YUCK"

subjected to various medical tests in places he called "chambers of horrors." Doctors put plastic tubes down his throat to test his stomach. Instead of regular food, they gave him an unpleasant pink liquid (Scott nicknamed it "YUCK") through these tubes.

For four years he suffered.

The turning point finally arrived in the third grade, when Dr. Andrew Klepner, a friend of the Hamilton family who was not one of the physicians working on Scott's case, took a special interest in the boy's troubles. Because Dr. Klepner suspected that the restricted diets and the awful pink liquid were doing more harm than good, he suggested an experiment. He offered to stay with the Hamiltons over a week-end and to watch Scott closely while

the boy ate whatever he wanted. That weekend Scott ate anything that tasted good, including ice cream made with milk. When there were no ill effects, Dr. Klepner sent Scott to the Boston Children's Hospital, where specialists discovered that the boy's stomach problems were caused by a

portion of his intestines that was not func-
tioning. As part of the therapy to overcome
this, they recommended exercise.

another turning point...

At the same time, another turning point
in Scott's life came when he accompanied
his sister Susan on a visit to an ice rink. Susan
was six years older and much healthier than
him, and she had great fun gliding on the ice
while he watched in amazement. Scott
excitedly told his parents that he wanted to
try skating.

...he wanted to try skating.

the path to glory

Scott was only nine when he first tried the ice. To start a new sport is difficult for anyone, but for a skinny, undersized boy who had spent four years hooked to tubes, the challenge was especially tough. It took dedication to keep going, to keep practicing after so many violent, painful falls on the cold, unyielding ice; but then Scott was already accustomed to pain and discomfort.

He suffered. Sometimes he cried. But he never stopped skating.

The benefits of his hard work showed up

during his next physical exam. Doctors had good news: Scott was finally growing again. His childhood illness was gone. "I skated myself out of it," he recalls.

The years without growth took their toll, however, and even today Scott stands only five feet, three and half inches tall. Because he was so small and had selected figure skating as his sport, Scott faced tough times at school, becoming a target for bullies. To show how strong he really was, Scott courageously signed up for his school hockey team, the Blackhawks, hoping his skill on the ice would give him an advantage over the larger boys.

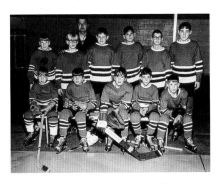

"I skated myself out of it . . ."

He was half right. Scott proved to be an excellent player and could outmaneuver most of the others, but his small size was a great disadvantage. One season he was hit

39

so hard that he spent two weeks with his neck in a brace. Clearly, hockey was not his sport.

At age thirteen Scott made the very tough decision to move away from his family and begin serious skate training in Illinois, under Coach Pierre Brunet. Although being separated from his loving and supportive family was difficult, Scott made the sacrifice to pursue what he felt he could do best. He was

rewarded just five years later, when he won the United States Men's Junior Championship.

But supporting Scott while he lived apart from them was a financial burden on his parents, and the next year they could no longer afford it. Scott agreed to come home to Ohio, to give up skating and attend college. At this point an unexpected benefactor stepped in. Coach Carlo Fassi, who had trained famous skaters such as Peggy Fleming and Dorothy Hamill, was impressed enough by young Scott's talent to find an outside sponsor who would pay the boy's expenses. Scott began training under Coach Fassi in Denver, Colorado, and placed respectably in several national and international events.

"Switching coaches is never easy. It's a harsh reality of the skating world."

When his mother died from cancer in 1977, Scott decided to honor her memory by trying harder. He moved to Philadelphia, Pennsylvania, and began training under Coach Don Laws. With his renewed commitment and the expert help of Coach Laws, Scott won third place in the 1980 Nationals and made the U.S. Olympic team. Although he only placed fifth in the Games, he describes carrying the American flag in that year's Olympic parade as the proudest moment of his life.

The next year at the National Championships, Scott earned two perfect

perfect scores

6.0 scores from the judges and won the men's singles. He went on to win the World Championships in 1981 and, despite a very troubled start in which he re-skated one program and fell during another, he also won the 1982 U.S. Championship. He also successfully defended his title again at the World Championships.

In 1983 he shook up the skating world by performing in a customized speed-skater's outfit instead of the traditional sequined suit worn by most male figure skaters.

He explained that he wanted his sport taken more seriously as a sport—to push it in a more athletic direction—and that this was the best way to do it. When he wore a similar costume during the Olympics next year, he changed the look of men's competitive skating forever.

the 1984 Olympics

The pressure on Scott was intense when he arrived in Sarajevo, Yugoslavia, for the 1984 Olympics. His health was compromised by a head cold and an ear infection, which affected his balance, but he kept this a secret until after the competition. Although his lack of balance created a problem during his leaps and spins, Scott scored so well in the earlier, less spectacular parts of the competition that he won first place in spite of his illness. It was the first time an American man had won a gold medal for Olympic skating since 1960.

Scott had remained unbeaten for four years, and he followed up his Olympic performance with a much more dramatic first place performance at the World Championships later that year, where he debuted his now famous soaring back flip. It was the final skate of his amateur career.

Scott was turning pro.

a star on ice

The same year that he won the Olympic gold medal, Scott joined the Ice Capades skating show, where he worked until it changed owners in 1986. When the time came to renew his contract, the Ice Capades' new management informed him that he would not be invited back. They felt that audiences did not buy tickets to watch male skaters. Scott set out to prove them wrong.

Joining forces with his friend Bob Kain at the International Management Group,

Scott created a show of his own called the
Scott Hamilton America Tour. Since he was
already friends with many famous skaters,
it was easy to get top stars to join him.
From a brief five-city run starting in late
1986, the show evolved into the annual
spectacular now called Stars on Ice.

Although the tour doesn't carry his name, Scott remains its coproducer and continues to skate in it every year.

More than a successful high-profile event, Stars on Ice has become an institution, drawing thousands of spectators at every city it reaches and being seen by millions more on TV. Unlike competitive events, where the order in which athletes skate is determined by a random drawing, Stars on Ice is a show where each element is carefully planned to be as entertaining as possible. Champion skaters love the freedom it gives them to use whatever music,

costumes, and movement they choose without the constraints of official rules and judges' tastes. Audiences love Stars on Ice because, quite simply, it offers more fun than competitive skating.

more fun

another challenge

In February 1997, while touring with Stars on Ice, Scott started suffering from abdominal pain once again. But this was very different from his old childhood illness, and it soon had him worried. In March he went to a doctor and learned the awful news: He had cancer—the same terrible disease that had taken his mother's life.

Scott was determined to fight it. He announced his condition publicly and said

"We're all capable

with confidence that he would "be back on the ice within a few months." Scott added, "Cancer is

something that can be overcome. I look at this episode in my life as just that—another episode and nothing more. We're all capable of rising above any obstacle."

of rising above any obstacle."

On March 21, he started a program of chemotherapy at the Cleveland Clinic Cancer Center, and thousands of cards, gifts, and well-wishes came pouring in from his fans. On June 24, doctors performed abdominal surgery to remove the cancer. Afterward, they found no active cells 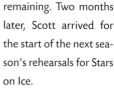 remaining. Two months later, Scott arrived for the start of the next season's rehearsals for Stars on Ice.

True to his promise, he was back.

a hero off the rink

Scott openly supports a wide range of charities, including the Make-A-Wish Foundation and other organizations that help children with severe medical conditions. The kids easily warm up to Scott, not only because he truly understands what life is like for them but because his small, boyish size sets them at ease.

Today Scott is more popular than ever, winning new fans each year. His upbeat commentaries for CBS Sports have already proved he can be a star outside the ice

rink, and he had already become an act-
ing/singing/dancing sensation in a 1989
Broadway show, but Scott's talents continue
to be expressed in new areas. He even has a
role in the movie *On Edge*, released in 2000,
and he has appeared in TV commercials driv-
ing a car on a sunny day—about as far from
the ice as he could be.

It is a proud testimonial to his endurance
and dedication that, even without skates, he
remains as popular with the public as he is in
the rink. With Olympic triumph behind him,
Scott Hamilton is a champion who continues
to grow—not in glory or size—but in spirit.

"We have given the best in the world a place to take their skating far beyond what they were able to do as competitive athletes. A place where we aren't presenting just skating but the best of what we are and hope to be. For you."

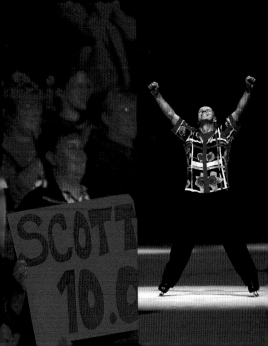

Scott

He Said/They Said

Scott's Quotes

"Slowing down is not my style, especially not when I was in the biggest competition of my life: Me versus cancer . . . 'What's the worst thing that could happen?' I said. 'That chemo[therapy] would cause the last three hairs on my head to fall out?' "

"Every day should be celebrated. Every day should be beautiful. You have to find a way."

"An Olympic gold medal is no barometer of who you are as a human being."

"Every lesson from every coach could be considered a brick in building something strong and lasting. Each competitor taught me how to test myself and gave me memories."

"If you are five-foot-two, there's nothing you can do about it. If you're six-foot-four, there's nothing you can do about it. If you're a little heavy, there's beauty in that, and if you're meant to be thin, there's beauty in that. That image of perfection we all aspire to applies, I think, to one in ten thousand people. And they're the ones modeling all the clothes in fashion magazines. I don't think I've met a person who doesn't have a list of things they have to deal with. My things just happen to be that I'm short and bald."

Their Quotes

"He's a champion on and off the ice, a great friend . . . someone I'll always look up to."
—*Tara Lipinski*

"He has always been a role model for me."
—*Brian Boitano*

"He made pro skating what it is today, and he's a sweetheart to boot."
—*Kristi Yamaguchi*

"It's been twenty-five years since a man won three World Championships, and

I would just like to say, this man is a
champion off the ice as well as on the ice."
—*David Jenkins (the last man to win three World
Championships before Scott Hamilton)*

"He has not only been a friend upon whom
I can always depend but an inspiration from
whom I have often drawn strength."
—*Ekaterina Gordeeva*

"Scott Hamilton is
Skate God for Life—
and that is no joke."
—*Kurt Browning*

Scott

Fact File

FULL NAME: Scott Scovell Hamilton

BIRTHDATE: August 28, 1958

HOME: Denver, Colorado

HEIGHT/WEIGHT: 5' 3 1/2", 115 lbs.

PARENTS: Ernest and Dorothy Hamilton

BROTHER AND SISTER: Steve and Susan

Scott's support team

CHOREOGRAPHER: Sarah Kawahara
COSTUME DESIGNER: Jef Billings

Scott's professional life

PRODUCT/COMPANY ENDORSEMENTS:
Target, Inc.
CHARITIES HE SUPPORTS: The Scott
Hamilton CARES (Cancer Alliance for
Research) Initiative, Target House at St.
Jude Children's Research Center, Athletes
Against Drugs, Pediatric AIDS, Make-A-
Wish Foundation

Scott's favorites

FOODS: Anything Asian! . . . then everything else.

MUSIC: Bruce Springsteen, Edwin McCain, The Rolling Stones, Aerosmith, Cheap Trick

SPORTS: Golf and bad golf

Scott

Awards and Achievements

amateur competitions

1st—The Winter Olympic Games 1984
1st—World Championships 1981, 1982, 1983, 1984
1st—U.S. Championships 1981, 1982, 1983, 1984
1st—Eastern Championships 1981, 1982, 1983, 1984
1st—Golden Spin of Zagreb 1983
1st—Skate America Championships 1982
1st—NHK Trophy 1982
1st—Skate America Championships 1981
1st—U.S. National Sports Festival 1981

1st—Skate Canada 1980
5th—World Championships 1980
5th—The Winter Olympic Games 1980
3rd—National Championships 1980
4th—National Championships 1979
1st—Norton Skate 1979
11th—World Championships 1978
9th—National Championships 1977
1st—National Junior Championships 1976
Last Place—Novice Nationals 1973

professional competitions

1st—Gold Championship 1994
1st—Canadian Professional Skating
    Championship 1994
1st—World Professional Championships 1984, 1986
1st—World Challenge of Champions 1986

other notable awards

★ U.S. Olympic Hall of Fame 1990

- ★ World Figure Skating Hall of Fame 1990
- ★ Jacques Favart Award 1988
- ★ Olympic Spirit Award 1987
- ★ Professional Skater of the Year 1986
- ★ U.S. Olympic Committee Athlete of the Year 1981, 1982, 1983, 1984

Scott's autobiography

Landing It: My Life On and Off the Ice by Scott Hamilton and Lorenzo Benet; 1999

Scott

How to Keep in Touch

STARS ON ICE WEB SITE: www.starsonice.com

MAILING ADDRESS:

—Scott Hamilton, c/o International Management Group (IMG), One Erieview Plaza, Cleveland, OH 44114

—Scott Hamilton, c/o Michael Sterling & Associates, 4242 Van Nuys Blvd., Sherman Oaks, CA 91403-3710

photo credits

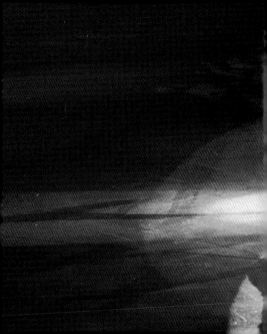